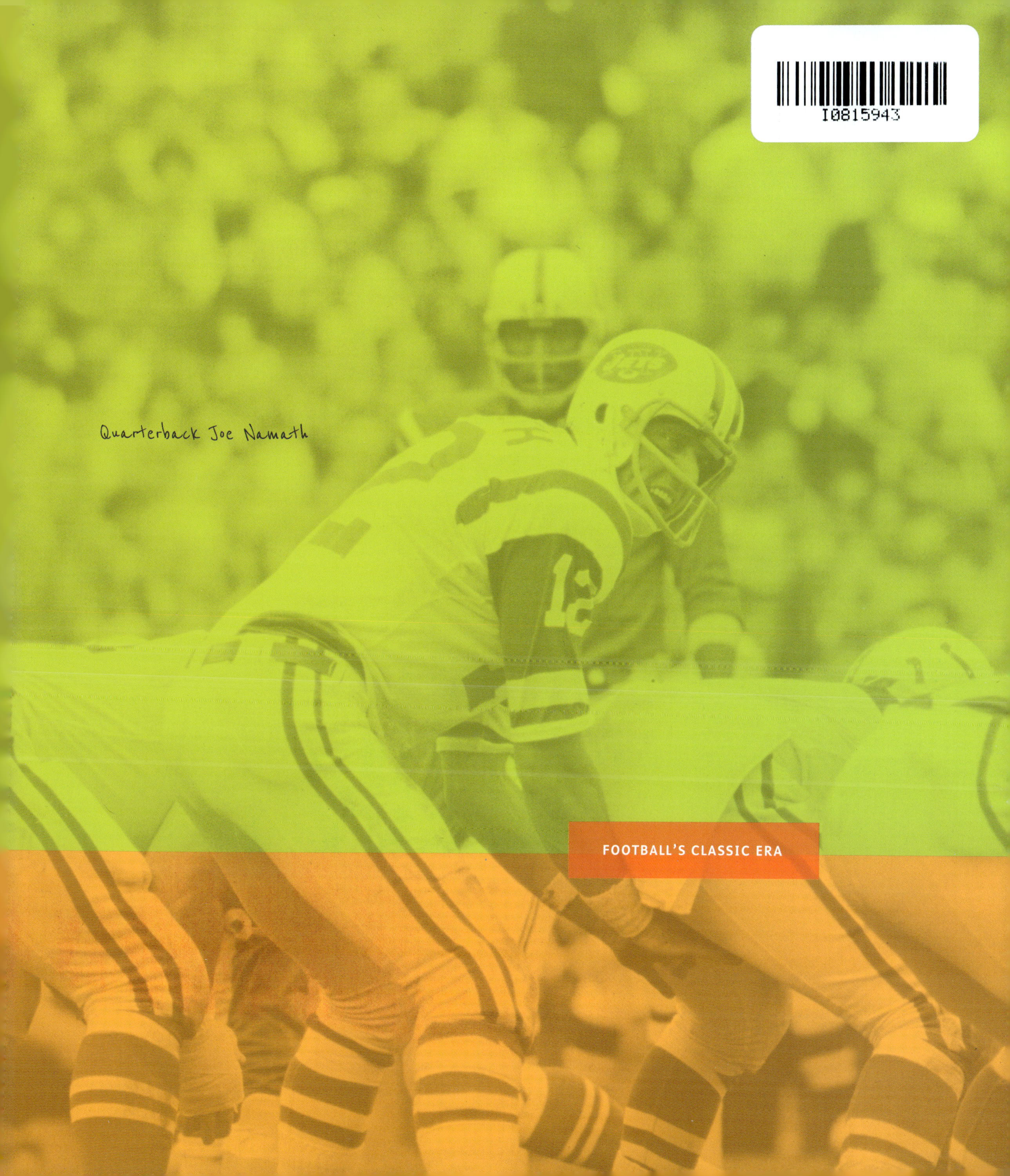
Quarterback Joe Namath
FOOTBALL'S CLASSIC ERA

Quarterback Roger Staubach

NFL SUPER BOWL STORIES

FOOTBALL'S CLASSIC ERA

(1967–1974)

JAMES BARRY

Head coach Vince Lombardi

CREATIVE EDUCATION / CREATIVE PAPERBACKS

Published by Creative Education and Creative Paperbacks
P.O. Box 227, Mankato, Minnesota 56002
Creative Education and Creative Paperbacks are imprints
of The Creative Company
www.thecreativecompany.us

Design and production by Blue Design (www.bluedes.com)
Art direction by Graham Morgan
Edited by Kremena Spengler

Images by Getty Images/Andy Hayt, 7, B Bennett, 28, Bettmann, 1, Bob Peterson, 10, George Gojkovich, 2, Focus On Sport, 6, 9, 12, 15, 16, 19, 25, 30, George Rose, 7, James Flores, cover, 11, Jon Soohoo, 6, Kidwiler Collection, 22, 31, Lee Balterman, 3, Otto Greule Jr, 7, Robin Alam/Icon Sportswire, 6, Robert Riger, 7, Ronald C. Modra, 20, 29, Walter Iooss Jr., 26–27; NFL/George Long/WireImage.com, 14, Rod Hanna/WireImage.com, 4–5, 32, Vernon Biever, 6, 10

Library of Congress Cataloging-in-Publication Data
Names: Barry, James (Author of children's books), author.
Title: Football's classic era (1967–1974) / James Barry.
Description: Mankato, Minnesota : Creative Education and Creative Paperbacks, [2026] | Series: Creative sports: NFL super bowl stories. | Includes index. | Audience: Ages 8–12 | Audience: Grades 4–6 | Summary: "Vince Lombardi, Don Shula, Bart Starr: Football's Classic Era (1967–1974) was dominated by these names. Dramatic recaps introduce middle-grade readers to star NFL players from this era and eight exciting Super Bowls"– Provided by publisher.
Identifiers: LCCN 2024051469 (print) | LCCN 2024051470 (ebook) | ISBN 9798889896074 (library binding) | ISBN 9781682777732 (paperback) | ISBN 9798889896876 (ebook)
Subjects: LCSH: Football–United States–History–20th century–Juvenile literature. | Football players–United States–History–20th century–Juvenile literature. | National Football League–History–20th century–Juvenile literature.
Classification: LCC GV950.7 .B372 2026 (print) | LCC GV950.7 (ebook) | DDC 796.332–dc23/eng/20241122
LC record available at https://lccn.loc.gov/2024051469
LC ebook record available at https://lccn.loc.gov/2024051470

Printed in India

Fullback Larry Csonka

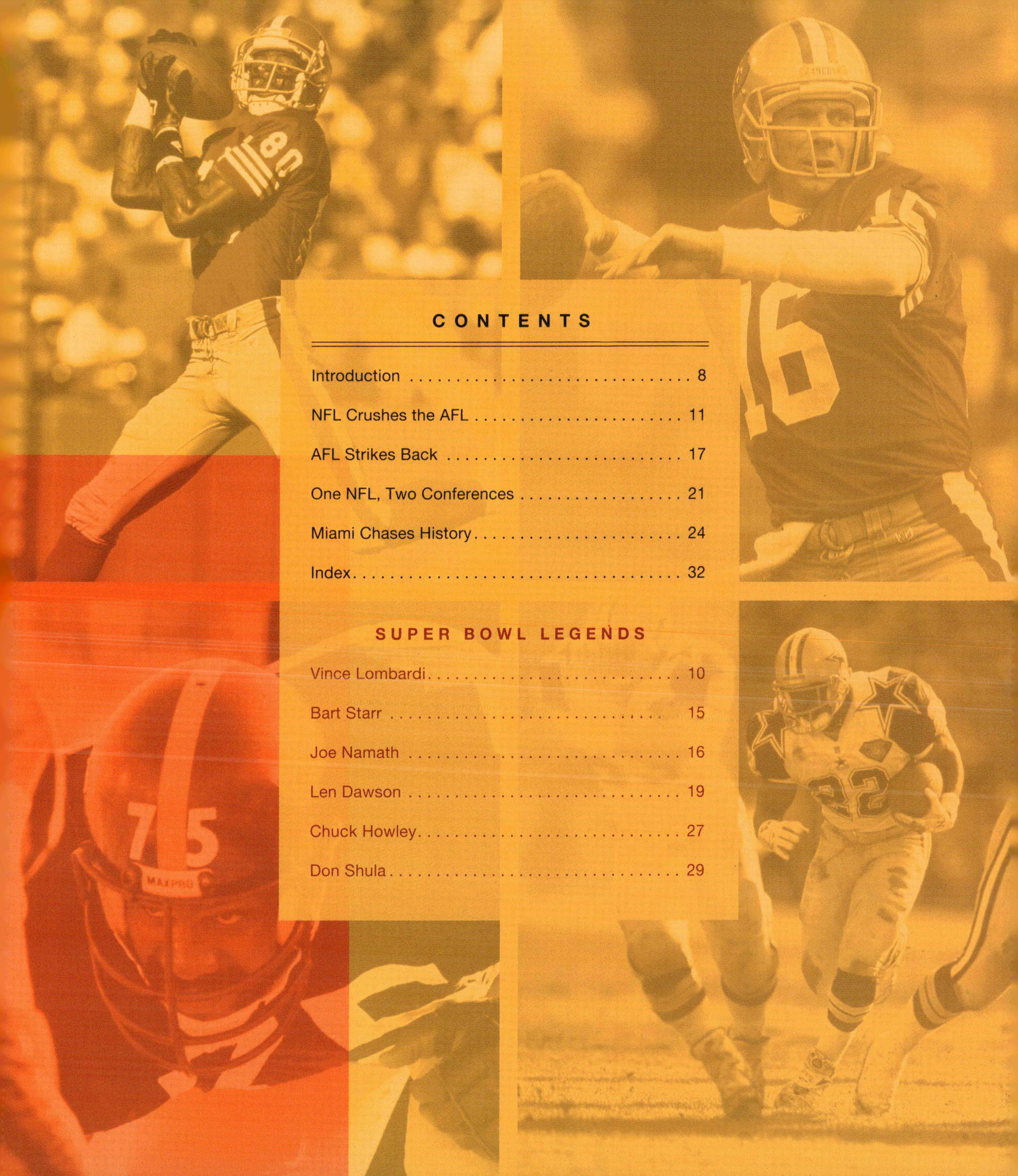

CONTENTS

SUPER BOWL LEGENDS

INTRODUCTION

It's the fourth quarter of Super Bowl V (5) at the Orange Bowl in Miami, Florida. There are under two minutes left. The score is 13–13. Dallas Cowboys quarterback Craig Morton drops back and throws a pass to running back Dan Reeves. It slips through his hands and bounces into the arms of linebacker Mike Curtis for an interception. Two plays later, the whole game rests on the shoulders of a rookie kicker. Baltimore Colts kicker Jim O'Brien lines up a 32-yard field goal with nine seconds left. Millions of Americans are watching. Colts fans are holding their breath. Cowboys fans are praying he misses. And it's good! O'Brien did it! The Baltimore Colts are Super Bowl champions.

Every football team wants to win the Super Bowl. It's the championship game between the best teams from each conference. The first Super Bowl was played in 1967. In the early Super Bowls, football looked very different from the game we see today. Football's "Classic Era" is filled with rich history and legendary names.

Kicker Jim O'Brien

VINCE LOMBARDI

HEAD COACH

GREEN BAY PACKERS, 1959–1967

Vince Lombardi was the winning coach of the first two Super Bowls. As head coach and general manager of the Packers, he turned a losing team into a dynasty. The Packers won one game in the 1958 season. In Lombardi's first season, the team improved to 7–5. Over the next eight seasons, they won five NFL Championships and two Super Bowls. Lombardi never had a losing season as a head coach in the NFL. Known for his inspiring speeches, he was one of football's greatest leaders. The Super Bowl trophy is named the Vince Lombardi Trophy in his honor.

Quarterback Bart Starr, Super Bowl I (1)

NFL CRUSHES AFL

The first Super Bowl was special. There was no single football league as we know it today. The American Football League (AFL) and the National Football League (NFL) had their own teams. They played in their own championship games. In 1967, the two leagues decided to see which had the best team. So the champion from each league faced the other in the first AFL–NFL World Championship Game. It was the AFL's Kansas City Chiefs against the NFL's Green Bay Packers. "Watch Super Coverage of the Super Bowl," the newspapers read. It was the first championship game of its kind.

The Chiefs met the Packers at the Los Angeles Memorial Coliseum in Los Angeles, California. Head coach Hank Stram and his Chiefs were known for their high-scoring offense. Quarterback Len Dawson was the top-rated passer in the AFL. Head coach Vince Lombardi and his Packers were an NFL power. They had won four NFL championships in six years. Veteran quarterback Bart Starr had just won the NFL Most Valuable Player (MVP) award.

The first half of the game was close. Green Bay scored first on a 37-yard touchdown pass from Starr to wide receiver Max McGee. The Chiefs tied the game with a 66-yard scoring drive in the second quarter. At halftime, the Packers led the Chiefs 14–10.

Kansas City advanced to midfield on their first drive of the second half. But on a third down, the Packers blitzed Dawson and forced an interception. Safety Willie Wood picked off the pass and ran all the way to the five-yard line. It was the play of the game. The Packers scored a touchdown, and the Chiefs never scored again. Green Bay won the first Super Bowl by a score of 35–10. Starr was named Super Bowl MVP.

Super Bowl II (2) saw Lombardi and his Packers return to another championship game. This time they faced the AFL champion Oakland Raiders. It wasn't as easy a road to this Super Bowl for the Packers. They had lost many key offensive players to injuries. They had finished the season with a record of 9–4–1. They had beaten the Cowboys in the NFL Championship with a close score of 21–17.

Most people believed the NFL teams were much better than the AFL teams. But the Raiders had finished with the best regular season record in AFL history at 13–1. They had won the AFL Championship by a score of 40–7. They led all AFL and NFL teams in scoring with 468 points. Quarterback Daryle Lamonica led the AFL with 30 touchdown passes. Future Hall of Famer Fred Biletnikoff was a great wide receiver.

Running back Elijah Pitts

The Raiders had a feared defense known as the "Eleven Angry Men."

Wide receiver Fred Biletnikoff

The two teams met at the Orange Bowl. On the first offensive play of the game, the Raiders handed it off to running back Hewritt Dixon. Packers linebacker Ray Nitschke tackled him for no gain. It was a hard hit that set the tone for the game. Green Bay led Oakland 3–0 after one quarter of play. Starr threw a 62-yard touchdown pass to wide receiver Boyd Dowler in the second quarter. The Packers led 13–0. Lamonica answered with a 23-yard touchdown pass of his own to wide receiver Bill Miller. The Raiders were still in it. After the first half, the score was 16–7.

The second half proved the fans and experts right. The Packers pulled away from the Raiders. The play that sealed their victory was an interception by cornerback Herb Adderley. He returned it for a 60-yard touchdown. Kicker Don Chandler made the extra point. Green Bay led Oakland 33–7 in the fourth quarter. The final score was 33–14. The first two Super Bowls belonged to Lombardi's Packers. The first two Super Bowl MVPs belonged to Bart Starr. The NFL had proven it was the better football league.

BART STARR

QUARTERBACK
GREEN BAY PACKERS, 1956–1971
6-FOOT-1, 197 POUNDS

Bart Starr led the Green Bay Packers to two Super Bowls and five NFL Championships. The Hall of Fame quarterback became Green Bay's starter in 1959. That was also the first season Vince Lombardi coached the Packers. Lombardi built a dynasty in Green Bay, and Starr was at the center of it. Starr was a great leader and an intelligent field general. He always stepped up his game in the postseason. In six NFL Championship Games, he threw only one interception. He won back-to-back Super Bowl MVPs. He was one of the greatest winners of all time.

JOE NAMATH

QUARTERBACK
NEW YORK JETS, 1965–1976
6-FOOT-2, 200 POUNDS

Joe Namath led the New York Jets to their first and only Super Bowl in 1969. Playing for a New York team, he earned the nickname "Broadway Joe." He famously guaranteed the underdog Jets would beat the NFL's Baltimore Colts before they won Super Bowl III (3). It was one of the greatest sports upsets of all time. In the 1972 season, he led the NFL in passing yards and passing touchdowns. Namath stood out on the field with his white shoes and his long hair. He was always known for his style and his confidence as much as his play.

AFL STRIKES BACK

Super Bowl III (3) was a matchup between the AFL champion New York Jets and the NFL champion Baltimore Colts. Again the NFL champion was expected to win. The Colts had completed an excellent season under head coach Don Shula. They finished with a record of 13–1. Veteran quarterback Johnny Unitas injured his throwing arm before the season. His replacement Earl Morrall had the best year of his career. Morrall led the NFL in passer rating during the regular season. The Colts offense ranked second in the NFL in points scored. Their defense ranked first with the fewest points allowed.

The Jets were led by head coach Weeb Ewbank. They finished the AFL season with a record of 11–3. Their defense allowed the fewest rushing yards in the league. Quarterback Joe Namath was so confident in his Jets team that he guaranteed they would win. An article quoting him in the *Miami Herald* made his guarantee famous.

The Jets met the Colts at the Orange Bowl. The first quarter proved the game wasn't such a mismatch. Neither team scored. Things changed early in the second quarter. Jets defensive back Randy Beverly intercepted a pass from Morrall. The following Jets drive led to a four-yard touchdown run from running back Matt Snell. Morrall threw two more interceptions in the quarter. The Jets gained control of the game. They led 7–0 at halftime.

The Jets grew their lead to 13–0 with two Jim Turner field goals in the second half. The Colts offense was struggling. The New York defense held it scoreless through three quarters. Coach Shula tried to boost his offense by replacing Morrall with Unitas. The veteran made some big passes. But it didn't matter. The Jets grew their lead to 16–0 with another field goal in the fourth quarter. The Jets beat the Colts by a final score of 16–7. The AFL had taken down the giants of the NFL. The Jets were Super Bowl champions. Namath's guarantee proved true. He was named Super Bowl MVP.

Super Bowl IV (4) may have been the biggest Super Bowl yet. The AFL had proven its worth by beating the NFL in Super Bowl III (3). With a win in this one, they could even the series. The AFL champion Chiefs were set to face the NFL champion Minnesota Vikings. Even though the Jets had just won the Super Bowl, people still thought the NFL was much better than the AFL. They thought the Jets just got lucky. Coach Stram's Chiefs returned to the big game on a mission to prove the doubters wrong. They wanted to avenge their loss in Super Bowl I (1).

The Vikings were led by head coach Bud Grant. They had completed a dominant season in the NFL. They led the league in points scored and fewest points allowed. Their defensive linemen were nicknamed the "Purple People Eaters." They were known for their tough, intimidating style of play. Quarterback Len Dawson was still leading the Chiefs offense. Kansas City also had a great defensive line. The Chiefs led the AFL in fewest points allowed. It was a matchup between each league's best defenses.

LEN DAWSON

QUARTERBACK
KANSAS CITY CHIEFS, 1962–1975
6-FOOT-0, 190 POUNDS

Len Dawson led the Kansas City Chiefs to one Super Bowl and three AFL Championships. He was known for keeping his cool under pressure. He earned the nickname "Lenny the Cool." Head coach Hank Stram often called him "the most accurate passer in pro football." He led the AFL in completion percentage seven times. In college at Purdue University, he played quarterback and defense. He was the team's kicker. Dawson did it all. But he'll always be known best for his victory in Super Bowl IV (4). The Chiefs' huge upset win over the NFL champion Vikings made football history.

Head coach Bud Grant

The two teams met at Tulane Stadium in New Orleans, Louisiana. There were nearly 81,000 people in attendance. Rain from the previous night left the field muddy. The Vikings struggled to move the ball at all. The Chiefs kicked three field goals in the first two quarters to take a 9–0 lead. Then Minnesota's Charlie West fumbled a kickoff return. Two minutes later, Mike Garrett scored a rushing touchdown. The Chiefs were up 16–0 at halftime.

In the third quarter, Vikings quarterback Joe Kapp led the team to a 69-yard scoring drive. Running back Dave Osborn finished it with a four-yard rushing touchdown. The score was 16–7. The Vikings were starting to come back. Then Dawson sealed the Super Bowl with the play of the game at the end of the third quarter. He completed a 46-yard touchdown pass to wide receiver Otis Taylor. The Chiefs went up 23–7, and the score stayed that way. They were crowned Super Bowl IV (4) champions. Dawson was named Super Bowl MVP. The AFL had evened the score at 2–2. Each league now had a pair of Super Bowls. Kansas City and the AFL had proven the doubters wrong.

ONE NFL, TWO CONFERENCES

uper Bowl V (5) was the first Super Bowl as we know it today. The NFL and the AFL had officially joined to form one league. All 26 NFL and AFL teams were split into two conferences with 13 teams each. They became the American Football Conference (AFC) and the National Football

WATERS
41
19

Conference (NFC). The Super Bowl became the NFL Championship Game. The AFC champion Baltimore Colts faced the NFC champion Dallas Cowboys. The two teams met at the Orange Bowl. It was the first Super Bowl played on artificial turf.

The game became known as the "Blunder Bowl." The Colts and the Cowboys combined for a Super Bowl record 11 turnovers. There were five turnovers in the fourth quarter alone. There were a record six interceptions in the game. Cowboys quarterback Craig Morton threw three interceptions in the last eight minutes. Colts quarterback Johnny Unitas had his own struggles. He threw two interceptions and lost a fumble. Cowboys linebacker Chuck Howley caught both interceptions. Unitas completed only three of nine passes for 88 yards.

The game was tied 13–13 in the fourth quarter. Two plays later, Jim O'Brien made the game-winning 32-yard field goal. The first modern-era NFL Championship Game may have been ugly, but the Colts didn't care. They were Super Bowl champions.

The AFC champion Miami Dolphins met the NFC champion Cowboys in Super Bowl VI (6). The game was played at Tulane Stadium. It was a matchup between two great coaches. Cowboys head coach Tom Landry went up against Dolphins head coach Don Shula. Dallas entered the Super Bowl with a reputation for losing big games. The Cowboys had just suffered an ugly loss in Super Bowl V (5). They had lost the 1966 and 1967 NFL Championship Games before the merger. The Dolphins were playing in their first ever Super Bowl.

Quarterback Johnny Unitas, Superbowl V (5)

The Cowboys dominated the game. The score was 10–3 at halftime. Miami didn't score in the second half. An interception thrown by Miami quarterback Bob Griese in the fourth quarter all but ended things. Cowboys quarterback Roger Staubach threw his second touchdown pass of the game. He was named Super Bowl MVP. Dallas won by a final score of 24–3. The Cowboys finally won their first Super Bowl.

MIAMI CHASES HISTORY

Super Bowl VII (7) was another matchup between the two conference champions. The AFC's Dolphins were set to face the NFC's Washington Redskins. But something was different this time. The Dolphins had a chance to do something special. They entered the Super Bowl with a perfect record of 16–0. They could complete the first undefeated perfect season in NFL history with a win over the Redskins. The two teams met at the Los Angeles Memorial Coliseum.

Don Shula was still coaching the Dolphins. He was still looking for his first Super Bowl victory. He had lost some big games in his career, so there was a lot of pressure on him to win this one. The Redskins were led by head coach George Allen. Their offense was led by quarterback Billy Kilmer. He was the NFL's highest-rated passer in the regular season. It was expected to be a close game despite Miami's perfect record.

Manny Fernandez and Vern Den Herder make a tackle during Super Bowl VII (7).

36
54

CHUCK HOWLEY

LINEBACKER

DALLAS COWBOYS, 1961–1973

6-FOOT-3, 228 POUNDS

Chuck Howley was a special athlete his whole life. He's the only person in West Virginia University history to play five varsity sports. He became the first defensive player to win Super Bowl MVP. He intercepted two passes and forced a fumble in the Cowboys' loss to the Colts. He is still the only player on a losing team to receive the MVP award. Howley and the Cowboys returned the next season and beat the Dolphins to win Super Bowl VI (6). He recorded a fumble recovery and a 41-yard interception in that one. He played his best in the biggest games.

Dolphins quarterback Bob Griese threw a 28-yard touchdown pass to wide receiver Howard Twilley. It was the first scoring play of the game. The Dolphins led 7–0 after the first quarter. In the second quarter, the Redskins drove the ball into Miami territory. Kilmer threw a costly interception. Two minutes later, the Dolphins entered halftime up 14–0. The third quarter went scoreless. It looked like the Dolphins' perfect season was a sure thing. They were 15 minutes away from making history.

There were under three minutes left in the game. Dolphins kicker Garo Yepremian lined up a 42-yard field goal attempt. But the kick was blocked and returned for a touchdown. The Redskins were right back in the game. The score was 14–7. With just over a minute left, the Redskins had the ball, and a chance to tie the game with a scoring drive. But the Dolphins defense held strong. They ended the game with a sack. Miami had done it! They were Super Bowl champions. They completed the first and only perfect season in NFL history.

Super Bowl VIII (8) saw the defending champion Dolphins face the Vikings. The game was played at Rice Stadium in Houston, Texas. It was Miami's third straight Super Bowl appearance. The Vikings offense was led by quarterback Fran Tarkenton. The team was led by head coach Bud Grant. They

Quarterback Bob Griese

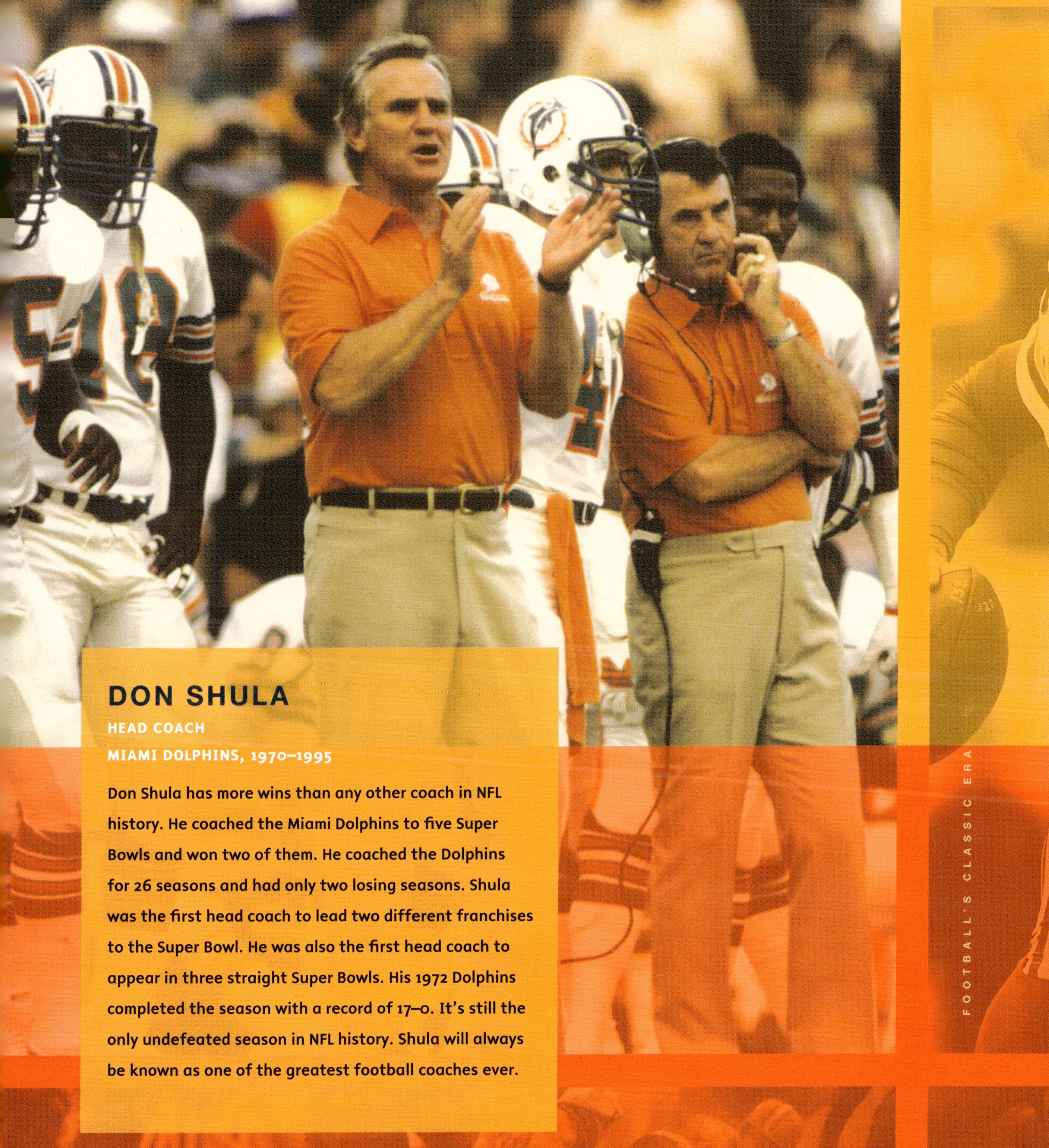

DON SHULA

HEAD COACH

MIAMI DOLPHINS, 1970–1995

Don Shula has more wins than any other coach in NFL history. He coached the Miami Dolphins to five Super Bowls and won two of them. He coached the Dolphins for 26 seasons and had only two losing seasons. Shula was the first head coach to lead two different franchises to the Super Bowl. He was also the first head coach to appear in three straight Super Bowls. His 1972 Dolphins completed the season with a record of 17–0. It's still the only undefeated season in NFL history. Shula will always be known as one of the greatest football coaches ever.

Quarterback Fran Tarkenton

weren't considered a tough match for the defending champs. Shula's Dolphins were on top of the NFL. They were expected to win again.

It was the most lopsided Super Bowl yet. The Dolphins led 24–0 through three quarters of play. Miami's rushing attack was too much for Minnesota's defense. Fullback Larry Csonka rushed for two touchdowns and 145 yards in the game. After his 33rd and final carry, coach Shula called him to the bench. Csonka limped off the field to a standing ovation. He was named Super Bowl MVP. The Dolphins won by a final score of 24–7. They were back-to-back Super Bowl champions.

The Classic Era was complete. Dynasties were built, and champions were crowned. A new era was on its way. The game would become extra physical. The toughest teams would usually win.

Fullback Larry Csonka, Superbowl VIII (8)

INDEX